Can Bugs

By Liza Charlesworth

ISBN: 978-1-339-02665-7

Art Director: Tannaz Fassihi; Designer: Tanya Chernyak
Photos © Getty Images and Shutterstock.com.
Copyright © Liza Charlesworth. All rights reserved. Published by Scholastic Inc.

3 4 5 6 7 8 9 10   68   32 31 30 29 28 27 26 25 24

Printed in Jiaxing, China. First printing, August 2023.

SCHOLASTIC

Bugs can sit.
But can bugs hop?

Yes! Hop, hop, hop!
Bugs can hop a lot.

Can cats hop? Yes!
Cats can hop on 2 legs.

Can bats hop? No!
But bats can flap.

Big rams can hop.

Tan dogs can hop.

Hop, hop, dip!
Frogs can hop and get wet.

Can kids hop? Yes!
Kids can hop a lot.